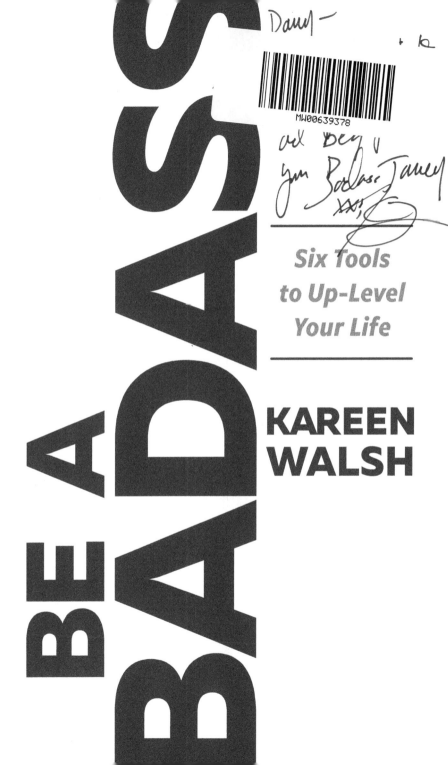

BE A BADASS

*Six Tools
to Up-Level
Your Life*

KAREEN
WALSH

Published by Revampologist, LLC

Printed in the United States of America

First printing, 2018

ISBN: 978-0-692-98626-4

eBook ISBN: 978-0-692-98627-1

For questions or more information, visit www.KareenWalsh.com/BeABadass

Book cover design, interior design, typesetting, and pre-press production by Lisa Von De Linde, LisaVdesigns.com

Editing by Alisia Leavitt Media, AlisiaLeavittMedia.com

TABLE OF CONTENTS

HOW TO LEVERAGE THIS BADASS BOOK

Are you afraid of change? Are you afraid that if you put yourself out there you might fail? For some people, facing the idea of change in their life is riddled with fear and anxiety based on a limited belief that they are don't deserve the life they dream of. I know, because I used to be that person. Even though I was labeled an over-achiever by people who observed me, on the inside, I did not believe I was worthy of fulfilling my dreams and creating a life for myself where I would thrive from the inside out. My journey, like most, started from the outside in. On the inside, I felt like a Lame-Ass.

What I mean by that is others' demands of me were more important than what I wanted for myself. The picture I had created of what a fulfilling life would be for me was not rooted in my desires, but a picture painted by others. I was never asked what I wanted, I was told what was best for me. It didn't work.

Fast forward down a twenty-year journey of self-discovery to overcome personal health challenges, broken relationships, obstacles in the career climb, and two failed start-ups, all leading me to build a thriving coaching/advisory practice where I help others achieve their badass lives. I do this by sharing the six fool-proof tools to up-level your life and be A BADASS IN TRAINING! I define a Badass in Training as someone who is willing to fail forward and put themselves out there to unapologetically achieve their Vision Life.

In this book, I share my journey through Badass Moments that shaped me, and the tools I used to help me create my Badass Life. I put this together to help YOU get into action towards your Vision Life and save time by leveraging these exercises I have used with my clients to create their Badass Life!

If you are looking for a shift in a specific area of your life or want to clearly identify what is holding you back, how to leverage your time, how to map out a plan to build the life you envision, and get into action to accomplish it, this book is for you.

When it comes to personal or professional development books, I learn better when information is presented to me because I can take notes, and I can put it into action myself. The best way to use this book is to read through and complete the exercise outlined in each chapter. You'll notice that every chapter builds on the one before, so I encourage you to be open and honest with what comes up as you go through the exercises. Trust the process, and reach out for help if you need it. I have many stories where leveraging these tools up-leveled not only my life but my clients' lives as well. I hope that sharing my methods of how I went from Lame-Ass to Badass helps you get into action towards the life you desire.

INTRODUCTION: A BADASS BEGINNING

I can remember it like it was yesterday: walking down Chestnut Street in San Francisco on a Saturday. It was one of my favorite areas of town to visit because the stores were so trendy, it was never crowded, and certain parts of the streets were elevated so high you could see the San Francisco Bay in the distance. It was a typical overcast day with the fog rolling in. I had just finished a pampered session of having a facial and a massage as a treat for hitting my latest promotion at my job. I was feeling relaxed and proud of my achievements as I started to walk past a jewelry store, and I found myself going in. I wanted to commemorate the moment where I first started to earn a base six-figure salary and had achieved a senior role in my firm with something. *Why not jewelry?*

I had never bought high-end jewelry for myself; most of what I had was gifted to me from my parents or family members. I honestly didn't know the price range of items like that, but thought if I could find something to remind me of my triumph and the courage I had to push myself to reach my goal, that would be badass!

The shop was fantastic—filled with sparkly items any women would swoon over—and I started to browse around. I felt like I didn't really look the part of someone who would purchase something there since I was in my workout gear post pampering session, had no makeup on, and wore nothing that would let a sales representative know I was a serious consumer. Maybe they would just let me look around and not bother me. As proud as I felt inside, I didn't feel like I looked the part in that moment. But, it didn't stop me from following through on my desire to celebrate.

As I looked in each case to find inspiration, I thought about the pavé diamond ring that I loved from Escada and had put on my vision board. (If you don't know what a vision board is, don't worry, you will learn about it in a few chapters.) The Escada ring was more of the wedding ring style, with a large diamond in the middle and a lot of pavé diamonds on the side. It was probably thousands of dollars, but it was so *me*: bold, beautiful, sparkly, and unique. I decided I wanted a white gold ring with diamonds on it. Just my luck, I found a white gold band that had inset diamonds scattered throughout and it was similar to a Tiffany stackable ring I liked. It fit my left pinky and was perfect!

"How much?" I asked.

"Seven hundred," the sale representative replied. I could tell she thought I was just trying things on and not serious about actually making a purchase.

"I'll take it."

I remember her being a bit surprised, then her customer service attitude turned on. "Why don't I have this cleaned right now? You can wear it out of the store," she said and whisked it away.

I was so full of pride that I was earning enough to throw down almost a thousand dollars without hesitation. It felt like a bold move. Gifting myself like this was new to me. I had earned this moment. I knew it would not be the last time I would celebrate like this.

I was only 28.

● ● ● ● ● ●

It was about four years prior that I had moved to San Francisco right after graduating college. I didn't really know anyone in San Francisco, but I knew I should try living in California before settling in New York. I packed two bags and moved to San Francisco where I had a cousin I could stay with who was the same age. He grew up in Southern California and I grew up in New York, but our personalities were so similar that we instantly clicked. He was so gracious to give me his bed while he slept on a mattress on the floor.

The house was near Golden Gate Park in the Richmond district closer to the Pacific Ocean. I remember the smell of the ocean, the dampness in the air, and foggy overcast mornings. He lived with three roommates and one had cats, which I was allergic to, so we had to keep the bedroom clean and the cats out. I knew I had to find other arrangements for the long term, but I made sure my cousin understood how grateful I was for letting me crash with him.

One skill I had learned over the years was how to put myself out there and network to find work. While living in my cousin's house, I still had to suit up, network with anyone who was willing, and find a Job. I knew that if I didn't find something by August, I would have to return to New York. When I had first left New York, my mother was not very encouraging about me moving across the US and said, "I will see you back here in August when this doesn't work out for you. Your room will be waiting."

Boy, that got me all fired up to succeed and prove her wrong!

When I would talk to her, I would act like everything was fine and I was making things happen. The truth was, I was exhausted, scared, and felt alone in my journey, but I still pressed on and relied on the certainty in my skills that I could make it work.

Prior to moving, I had reached out to my family friends and contacts from high school and college, saying I was moving to California and asked if they had connections I should meet with when I arrive. I discovered the parents of a friend of mine from my High School now happened to live in San Francisco. They were the most gracious couple. We met for brunch in Sausalito, California at a beautiful seafood restaurant on the water. They said if I needed anything to help in my transition, to reach out to them and treated me like they would want others to treat their kids. After reaching my level of discomfort at my cousin's house, I called them to see if I could stay with them for a few days while I worked on other arrangements. They welcomed me into their home and agreed to a maximum of a ten-day stay. I was so grateful I had somewhere to go.

At the time, they were living in a corporate apartment rental provided by the firm my friend's Dad was working for. He was an executive vice president at a renowned bank. It was a magnificent two-story penthouse apartment near Coit Tower. It reminded me of the home I grew up in—and a lifestyle that seemed so far in the distance since I left for college. It was also a total 180 degrees from the house I had just stayed in with my cousin.

It was such a unique dynamic to be living hand to mouth in my own life and have the rich experience of staying at my friend's parents' apartment while I looked for work. I will never forget how embarrassed I was when his mom asked me if she could put my suitcase in the garage and offered to pay to dry clean all my clothes because they came with a smell that she did not want lingering in her house.

I was mortified.

I guess during the first days of my new adventure in California, the odor of humidity and cats had permeated my clothes and suitcase. I made sure to get everything cleaned and told her to store my suitcase wherever she saw fit. I knew it would be best to figure out another place to live while I was apartment hunting, as I did not want to take advantage of their kindness.

● ● ● ● ● ●

About five days into staying with them, after going to different interviews pounding the pavement trying to find work, I landed a temp job at an art college. I was so excited that I would earn money again soon! The job was to start in a week. That Sunday, the family was out for the day and I sat in the living room that overlooked the San Francisco Bay on one side and hills on the other. I had laid out the Sunday classifieds on the floor trying to find an apartment that I could afford to rent. I started to cry. I remember thinking I would never find an apartment in my price range. I did not want to return to New York as a failure. I only had $1,500 in the bank that I had saved from college jobs and graduation gift money. I knew I would need it all to secure an apartment; first month, last month, and a deposit was the norm to sign a lease.

There was a studio apartment for rent that was $495/month and not in the best of neighborhoods at the time, but if I could get it I would make it my home. The temp job I had was paying $15/hour, which after taxes was about $390/week. The price point of this apartment was perfect! Everything else I saw was way more which would have stressed me financially. I had to have this place!

I circled the listing and put stars around it with my black sharpie. It said there was an open house scheduled that Monday. On the bus ride there, and the walk over to the apartment, I remember saying to myself, "Please be a clean and decent place that is safe for me to come and go from. Please still be available for me to rent. Please, please, please, this must work for me." I got to the address, found the security code for the building manager on the box, and buzzed and buzzed, but the apartment manager did not answer. All I got was voicemail. The apartments were above retail shops. It was a plain, taupe-colored four-story walk up.

I stepped into the bodega that was below the apartments. It sold mainly alcohol, cigarettes, beverages, essentials like bread and toilet paper, and some snacks. The woman behind the counter had a huge smile with short curly hair and said, "Hi Bay-bee, how can I help you?" with a bit of a southern accent I did not expect.

"Hi, my name is Kareen. I came to look at the apartment for rent upstairs, do you know the building manager? Have you seen him or others coming to look at the apartment today?"

"Nice to meet you. I'm sorry, I haven't seen anyone there today." She could sense my disappointment. The ad had said there was an open house at a specific time. I was there at that time and he was not." "You can hang out here if you want and wait for him." At that moment, a tenant from the building came into the store. "Have you seen the building manager of your apartment today? This woman is waiting for him."

"No, I haven't," the tenant said and turned to me. "I'm happy to let you in with me so you can see if the apartment is unlocked. If it isn't, you are welcome to take a peek at mine. They are practically the same unit." She happened to live in an apartment on the floor below the one I was coming to see.

My eyes widened. "Thank you so much!" I said and followed her out. I could not believe how nice and helpful everyone was there. I knew it would be the best place for me! It was the only place I had found at that price and in a somewhat decent area. And the welcome from the two ladies also gave me a sense of belonging and safety that I may not have felt if the building manager was my only guide to see the apartment. It was across the street from Section 8 housing, and if you turned down the wrong street within a five-block radius, you might see some things you would rather forget. But the price was right and I had to have it. I was determined to connect with the building manager and rent it.

I kept calling the building manager until he called me back. I finally got to see the apartment which was a studio but had a ten-step hallway that in the middle that split up the kitchen from the bathroom so it felt larger than the 300 square feet that it was. It was on the inside of the building, so it didn't have a view, only overlooked other apartments. It was perfect. I filled out the application and gave the building manager my resume. He said he would review it with the owner, and they would decide if I was a good fit. I told him I had first and last month's rent ready and to let me know if they needed any other information for me to secure the lease. He called me two days later, I got the place!

By August, things started to come together for me to stay in San Francisco. Now that I had the apartment and temp job, I still had to find a full-time job that represented my potential and a place for me to grow. I updated my resume with my current position and realized at the time that hiring managers were overlooking my resume because I did not have local experience. I redistributed my resume to all the prior job submissions I had made with my temp job included. I remember being told when I moved out to San Francisco not to expect to make more than $25,000 a year as a recent undergraduate from business school. However, I also remember thinking, *Watch me, I will make more.*

Within five weeks of moving into my apartment, I landed a full-time job as a Loan Documentation Specialist for Wells Fargo Bank. It was a glorified filing job, to say the least, but it paid $30,000. I took it. I remember my pride of making $5,000 more than expected. I stayed in that job for less than a year before I moved into another role at Wells Fargo as a Systems Analyst. I knew nothing about their technology, but I had technical aptitude from the few courses I took at George Washington University (GWU) while in business school. I impressed the VP of the department with my willingness to learn on the job and somehow, she decided to extend me an offer...for $38,000!

By this time, I was getting the hang of living in San Francisco and my commute to work. I was still in the same apartment, sleeping on a Full-size mattress that rested on the box spring on the floor. It had been a year in that apartment when my best friend from college moved to San Francisco and we decided to find a two-bedroom apartment together. Since I now had a steady income making around $3,000/month before taxes, I could spend more on our next place. This was when the .com boom started to happen, so apartment hunting was intense and competitive in '98. My bestie would do the apartment hunting while I was at work in between her interviews to find herself a full-time job. I made sure she had a packet of our information, a picture of us, and our resumes for the application process so if she found the right place, she could apply and humanize us on paper with the additional information I gave her in the folder.

One day, I was at my desk working away answering client inquiries and setting up plans for work across the support team, when my friend called me crying.

"What's wrong? Are you ok?" I asked.

"Fifty people just showed up to an apartment I just saw. It's perfect for us, Kareen," she said. "It has the right amount of space and the commute isn't that bad to downtown."

"Do we want the place?" I said, calmly.

"Yes, we want it," she replied. "I submitted our application with the folder we had put together and the realtor showing the place just ended up putting *everyone's* application in there. There's no way we are going to stand out now." Her voice was panicked.

"Get her card and come to the office. We will get this place!" I said with determination.

The realtor's office was two blocks away from the apartment. When I had called to make an appointment to come see her about the apartment, she didn't speak much English and was representing the owners of the building who no longer lived in the area; they were remote landlords. *Perfect*, I thought. *We just need to give them more information about us to show how responsible we are.* We drafted a letter about our backgrounds and how grateful we would be for renting the apartment. It was three blocks away from Golden Gate Park, and about a 25-minute bus ride to downtown on the express bus.

Since I had not seen the inside of the apartment, I completely trusted my friend's opinion. I brought my checkbook, in case I needed to put down a deposit. I had no idea what to expect as I entered the office. The woman was a hot mess and had all the applications in the folder we had given her, totally disorganized across a conference table. While she was talking, I kept eye contact with her as I took our folder and put our information and application with the letter together inside. I made sure to separate the other applications into a separate stack. I handed back the folder and then said to the woman, "What does the landlord need to know about us in order to choose us? What can we do to secure the apartment?"

"If you are that serious, leave a $300 check as good faith towards the deposit of the apartment, and I will get back to you on Sunday. It is between you and one other woman who has a baby and is moving here from out of state," she replied.

"I am sure the landlord will appreciate knowing that my banking and job is here in San Francisco and she does not have to worry about the transition of accounts from another state," I said, giving her the talking points I had hoped she would share with the landlord so the decision would be easy.

My friend and I were a wreck that weekend trying to distract ourselves and kept praying that we would get the place. We were starting to feel like we didn't get it. I kept visualizing the outside of the apartment and saying, "It will be ours! I can see us there." Then, the phone rang. We got it! This was another example of how my determination and badass skills helped me get what I wanted in life.

● ● ● ● ● ●

Fast forward five years: I was 28 and living in San Francisco for the second time due to a relocation demand from my firm. I had lived in New York through 9/11 and in Denver, Colorado as the strategic leader to oversee streamlining operations and team management for a company that my firm had acquired. I was now a senior manager for mergers and acquisitions operations for a financial software company that had started to acquire data reconciliation services platforms and teams.

I was one of two female senior technical process leaders under the CTO's organization. Thirty-three people were under my management. I had paved my way into a lucrative role that was unique to others in the firm. I started at $35,000 and worked up to a $115,000 base salary in less than five years. My total compensation with options and bonuses was upwards of $145,000 per year! I had lived between San Francisco, New York, and Denver for three years and was well respected by the executive team.

Looking back now at that point in my career, as a female leader in technology working for a female CTO and CEO, I was very fortunate to have the experience I did, no matter how hard it got. I grew from every risk I took, every person I interacted with, and the challenges they gave me. In order to succeed in the firm, I gave it all of me. I had previously worked for a company where although I gave it my all, it left me in a health crisis and underappreciated. I hit a glass ceiling at age 23 and resigned from that position to pursue a better fit for my skill set and a company I could grow within.

I learned that no one has control over my earning power, except for me. If I don't ask for what I want, I can't assume someone is going to just give it to me.

• • • • • •

When I joined the firm that allowed me to grow, earn, and learn, I made sure to understand the internal workings of the company. I took risks asking for what I wanted every time they gave me more to work on. I said yes to big challenges and stretched myself to prove I was capable. I mapped out my goals for my corporate ladder climb, and I managed to get a promotion and raise every six months. I had proven my worth each time and built efficient procedures and teams to manage daily operations, so I could continue to be strategic and help the company grow.

My first direct hire while working at this firm was around six months into the role. I had outlined the sales fulfillment and subscriber services required to maintain the business I was brought in to help run. The VP of sales approved my plan and allowed me to hire for help. It was similar to a customer support role with a strong understanding of process management but truly was an entry-level job that I would have to train someone for who was willing to learn.

I had started to build my relationship with the HR team to learn how to get the job posted and start recruiting for the position, determine salary range, etc. One of the HR administrators was a sweet, young lady. We would see each other sometimes at the gym after work and catch up while she would sprint on the treadmill and I would walk briskly beside her. She had the most contagious smile and great personality.

One day, I saw her running her heart out on the treadmill and crying! I was shocked and asked her if I could help her with anything. She said she was so miserable in her role at her job and that she was thinking of moving because San Francisco didn't seem right for her. I tried to console her and asked her what type of work would she like to be doing.

"I don't know," she said. "I'm only a year out of college, so I have a lot to figure out."

"If I have a job open on my team, would you consider coming to work for me? It will get you out of the department you are and try another role before quitting and moving home," I said. I remember her eyes widened with a hint of excitement. It would be so much fun to work together.

"Really?" she said.

"I'll do my best to make it happen," I replied with a smile. "We may need to finesse it since it is an internal transfer, but if you are willing, I am."

"Yes!" she said.

I got it all in motion. She was my first direct hire and the inspiration behind my *Badass in Training* (BIT) program that inspired me to write this book and share my refined methods with you. I remember writing up my first BIT manual (except back then it was the other B-word because that is what some people thought of me when I did not concede to their way and challenged them). She needed to learn the ropes and to understand how to create boundaries around what she would say yes to, and how often; how to prioritize her work and present tradeoffs when she had competing priorities. The main part of the training was to help her be assertive and voice her needs in order to complete specific tasks to please our client base, internally and externally. I did my best to teach her everything I knew so she could one day replace me and I could move onto the next role.

She found her voice and strengths in her new role. Eventually, she outgrew it and returned home to build a thriving career with a large retailer. I recently reconnected with her, almost seventeen years after we last worked together, and it was like no time had passed. It was so great to hear how she is thriving in her life and has designed it in a way that suits her and her family.

● ● ● ● ● ●

The program is called *Badass in Training* because I believe we always have something to learn, and a Badass recognizes not only where they shine but where they may need to put a little more effort to master a skill, and then how to build others up around them so they can move forward into the next level of life they plan to achieve. This is the foundation of this book.

Eventually, I resigned from my position at the firm. I realized I had achieved the corporate climb I had envisioned. Financially, I was stable. I bought a house in Denver, Colorado that I knew I could afford if I only made half of my income, so I could invest in other areas of living like my health, spiritual connection, relationships, and dig deeper into the type of mark I wanted to leave on others. I was on the cusp of turning 30 and simply wanted more. I took the plunge and started over. (*You can always be where you are today, so why not try?*)

This was the first time I attempted self-employment and worked from contract to contract after moving to Denver. I was able to focus on my health, master a few lucrative skills and invest in certain certifications so I could continue to attract new clients and projects to work on. With the extra income I earned, it was time to invest in myself. First on my list was self-care, then building a healthy relationship and connecting with my spiritual side. Together, these ensured I could lead a life where I was no longer in Survival Mode.

- **Survival Mode** is living hand to mouth and in conditions that do not quite yet represent the life you are working so hard for.
- **Maintenance Mode** is when you have built a satisfactory life, the ability to put a little away, but you still have to watch what you spend on in order to make sure the bills are paid each month and you are not increasing your credit card debt.
- **Living Mode** is when you have your bills paid with ease, you are able to save a good amount each month for the future, and still purchase what you want when you want it because you know you have the means to do so.

When I could visualize what I wanted, I was able to put intention behind it, and focus my actions to achieve it. I had a goal. I outlined my actions. I followed through. I didn't realize these innate habits to achieving what I wanted was a skill I would eventually teach others. A bit of fearless action to push yourself through discomfort and achieve the life you want has become the foundation of my thriving coaching practice today.

I believe your 20's is the time to say YES and try as much as possible, push your limits, and learn what you are all about to start to build the life you want in your 30's and beyond. I was persistent and bold in my 20's; I had nothing to lose. My mantra at the time was: *You can always be where you are today, so why not try?*

● ● ● ● ● ●

Today, I have a thriving strategic consulting firm, an executive and leadership coaching practice, a health and wellness business, and am about to cross off my goal of earning $1 million dollars in revenue in 2017. Most importantly, I am helping others earn six figures in their respective careers. I share this with you because I would not have been able to earn this amount annually if I did not follow the information you are about to read.

After years of experience building, running, leading, and coaching teams and leaders on how to perform at their best, I have refined the lessons and built a six-step book. If followed and repeated time and again, it will help you not only succeed in the career you dream of, but achieve the thriving life you desire as a whole.

Throughout this book, I will be sharing personal experiences as examples of how I apply the lessons, tools, and skills learned through the BIT method. You will understand more about how I leveraged each failure and triumphed in other areas of my life at times where the income was not present, but my life was more fulfilling than ever before. My goal is to have each of you learn something new that up-levels your life and gives you the clarity you need to find fulfillment in all endeavors, but most of all let go of the activities that no longer serve you.

I will introduce each session with a lesson learned and offer exercises to apply to your own life. As you continue through the book, each exercise will build on the previous. I like to keep things simple and practical, but it doesn't always mean it is easy. If you are uncomfortable or reach points of overwhelm, I would recommend reaching out to me or scheduling a 30-minute session so I can help you break through barriers and find the tools to keep you in action towards your Vision Life.

Why Badass?

BADASS to me is an acronym for my I AM statements. Each chapter in this book leads with a mantra statement and is to be repeated as you go through each exercise.

Mantras:

I am BOLD.
I am ASSERTIVE.
I am DRIVEN.
I am ALIGNED.
I am SELF-CONFIDENT.
I am SUCCESSFUL.

I AM BADASS.

Now, let's begin.
- Kareen Walsh

CHAPTER 1

I AM BOLD.

Being bold is probably the best way to describe my energy when I am about to take a leap into something new. I have no idea what I am doing but know if I don't try and put myself out there, I will never know. From a young age, I was a conduit for change and connection, inspiring others to go after what they wanted: showing them the way by leading by example, lending an ear, and helping them come up with solutions. Some of it was my natural empathetic and creative energy, and some of the skill came from breaking through my own unhealthy patterns and the desire to rid myself of emotional pain.

People have told me that moving to San Francisco at age 23 was a bold move. They often say how courageous I was to just set out and start my life there without a clear plan. I only had a vision of what I *thought* my life would be like if I didn't do it. For me, the shift from *What if?* to *I must!* became easier over time as I continued to make bold moves in the direction I thought was right.

Become the Architect of Your Vision Life

The person I am today is not that person I was twenty years ago, thank God! Yes, I can downgrade to an older version of myself, but is that optimal for the life I have today? Like your smartphone system upgrades, with everything we do, learn, interact with, and let go, we fix bugs and become new versions of ourselves. This helps to create a better experience, enhance our output and connection, and build new habits using the skills we have acquired. And with each growth spurt through life's lessons, we start to dream and visualize our lives in a different way. I do believe there is a season for everything, and in my pursuit of personal and professional development, I have learned from many who have mastered the ability to unleash their inner desires and get into action. *But first, you need to know where you are going, and why you want it so bad.*

I shared my energy of determination in the opening of this book to show you what it takes to focus on the end goal and make sure you get into action towards achieving it. Before we get into HOW we do it, we need to get clear on what we want! The difference in the version I am today vs. the version of myself twenty years ago, is that young girl was *only visualizing how to survive*, and this version of me *visualizes how to thrive*.

My 20's were all about taking risks and pushing myself because I had nothing to lose. I was pining to survive and was living hand to mouth until that moment in the jewelry store on Chestnut Street when I felt like I had made it. What came next shaped how I made bold moves to build the life I have today. The months after that Badass Moment became reflective and I questioned everything.

I would ask myself: *Is this where I want to be? Do I really connect with the work am I doing or is this just for the money? Are the people I work for people I want to become as I continue to climb the ladder? Have I reached a plateau? Is this all this opportunity has to offer? Is San Francisco right for me? What do I really want out of life? What kind of impact do I want to make? Could my health be better? What about relationships? Do I want to get married and have kids now that I have proven I can be successful in business?*

● ● ● ● ● ●

The list of questions went on and on, and each day I would journal to try to dig deep and figure out what was next. I had lived in Washington, DC, Manhattan, Denver, and San Francisco, and was questioning what I was doing it all for. I was getting close to 30, not in a stable relationship, restless in my daily routine, and just felt like there was more for me to put my time against. Like what I had done with each move prior, I mapped out what I wanted.

I mapped out my vision for the next phase in life. I made sure it was not just career focused. Why? Because I had built a certainty in my skill set and knew that I had proven I could make the money I needed to live the life I wanted. Now, I had to design the life I wanted to make the effort worth it. This is how I created my Vision Life, and I continue to check in and revise it whenever I feel stuck, even to this day.

When I first started this process, it was not as refined as it is now. I would create simple lists of things I wanted to achieve, feel, be, and do. It would look something like this:

- Move to Colorado and buy a house before quitting my job so I could get a mortgage with ease.
- Make sure the mortgage is half my current income in case I can't make the same amount in Colorado.
- Fall in love with a man that I can build a family with.
- Get healthy—lose 20 lbs.
- Save three months' income in case it takes time for me to find another job.
- Quit my job at a time where they will not only pay my salary, but incent me to stay longer by paying me a bonus.
- Start making connections in Denver and ask people who they might know to connect me with.
- Update résumé.
- Book weekends to go house hunting in Denver to see what I can afford.
- Start grooming one of my direct reports to take over my job when I leave (without them knowing I am leaving).
- Book a fun trip over the holidays to do something different before I find the next job in Denver.
- Communicate plan to friends and family for support.

I was very action oriented because it was what I did in my work life, so I applied the same tact to my personal life. But, do you see how there is no color to it? Do you see how robotic it feels? That was exactly how I would describe that version of me. I was orderly, organized, methodical, and driven. Yes, there are bold moves in there. And yes, I did achieve 90% of the list within four months. What I didn't realize is that I would still be in a state of flux once I achieved everything, because I didn't have a *defined* reason why I was doing all of it.

At that time in my life, my *why* was to SLOW DOWN! I wanted to find the time to take care of myself and interact with others who could uplevel me into a more connected version of myself, but I didn't know how to articulate that. I didn't know how to dream when I preferred to ground myself in what I could control.

Controlling everything was me in Survival Mode.

If I could control it, then I knew I could do something about it. And if it failed, I only had myself to blame. I didn't realize that living in the reactive space of controlling everything made me say yes to too many things that really didn't better my life. It was just more to do. I was not clear on my vision of how I wanted my life to be, and was bogged down with doing extra stuff that blocked my mind from letting the dreamer out. I had to let go, and find the pace to dream big again.

This is your first step: taking the time and space to dream big and map out your vision–then we will move into assessing how far you are from achieving that version of your life.

Tool #1: Getting Crystal Clear on the Life You Truly Desire

Start by answering the following questions in a free-from writing exercise. I know it may sound too simple, but it is! Trust me and write the answers to the following down on a few sheets of paper, or request the *Be A Badass: Six Tools to Up-Level Your Life Workbook* from my website to centralize all your learnings from this book in one place. Don't rush this process, and do it in a space where you can be open with your thoughts and keep writing. Feel free to explore more of your own questions beyond what I list here.

Some questions to ask yourself to get the ball rolling:

- When you daydream, what comes up for you?
- What do you wish your life was like?
- What do you desire most?
- How does it smell, taste, and feel? Who is with you? Where are the places you choose to go?
- Whose life are you impacting?
- What adventures do you go on?
- Where do you travel? Are they short or long vacations? Are you traveling for work?
- What clothes are you wearing? What does your home look like? Where do you see yourself shopping?
- What kind of food are you eating?
- How are you growing into the next version of yourself? Are you investing in programs to up-level the areas you want to improve upon?
- What do your finances look like?
- How do you earn an income? Are you working for yourself or others?
- What is your ideal physical strength/health?
- What is your body capable of doing?
- What kind of people are you attracting into your life? Who are you surrounding yourself with?
- Who are you in an intimate relationship with? Do you have a family? What are your kids like? What kind of experiences do you have together.
- What do you like to eat? Do you cook your own food, or does someone else cook for you?

Think about all areas of your life and how you want each to feel and be. Write it out. Don't rush this process. You can even use each question in a daily journal entry so you can focus on your answer. Add as much color as you can to really describe what the answer means to you. You may even rewrite your answer a few times as it gets clearer and clearer to you what you truly desire out of this precious life you have.

Your Vision Life is all yours! When you get clear on what you visualize it to be, then you can intentionally achieve it with an open heart and mind. But without a clear vision, you will run in a circle. Now that you have put statements down around each area of your life and how you visualize it, go back through what you have written. Highlight the most valuable ones that are critical to your desired life, then rewrite those statements starting with, "I am..."

For example, if you previously wrote:

I find the man of my dreams. He is a generous man who is connected to his family and has a fun network of friends that care about him and call to hang out often. We love to travel together and explore new destinations. He proposes in the most romantic way that makes me certain I have met someone that loves me and we can grow together. We get married and in the next seven years, we have two beautiful kids and live in the suburbs of Chicago close to our friends and family. The friends that surround us lift our spirit and always are up for hanging out on Sundays.

● ● ● ● ● ●

An "I am" statement could be:

- I am open to new relationships where I connect with others and share what I have on a regular basis to create new memories with my family and friends.
- I am a loving person who reciprocates the love I receive from others.
- I am a fun person who likes to hang out with the people I love.
- I am excited to learn from my friends and their experiences.

- I am confident that I will stand in my truth of how I am feeling in each new relationship so I can attract the man of my dreams with ease.

● ● ● ● ● ●

When you write "I am" statements out, they complement your Vision Life writing exercise and help you emote what you are truly wanting to become or already are. I find it grounding, even if right now your life doesn't reflect the "I am" statements in action. If you stick with this book and continue to go through the exercises, in the end you will be able to say these statements with certainty. I want you to write them out now as you are visualizing your Vision Life, because this will all act as your North Star to achieving the life you want.

If you get into moments of doubt or overwhelm, remember the Mantra: **I am Bold**. It takes a bold energy to dream big and start to architect your Vision Life. You can also create a vision board. Previously, I mentioned that I would put together imagery of what I wanted, liked, and desired onto a vision board. After doing this exercise, I suggest you put one together that represents the life you envision. Grab photos of the home life, wardrobe, car, friend, family, quotes, travel destinations, people you impact, causes you support—whatever represents the life you dream—and put them on a board. Place your vision board somewhere in your house where you see it every day. If you are more digital, Pinterest is a great app to build your vision board. Now that you have a clearer vision, let's move into the next step on assessing what you need to do to live it daily!

CHAPTER 2

I AM ASSERTIVE.

Being assertive is standing behind what you believe, no matter what. Imagine standing in your Vision Life. Feel it as if you are already there; embody it. As you look at where you stand today and where you plan to be, repeat **I am Assertive** in moments of doubt that pull you away from the level of satisfaction you want. This will help pull you forward into your Vision Life with ease. *When you are assertive when it comes to your true desires, you are unstoppable.*

Outlining the Blueprint of Your Biggest Badass Dreams
A strong foundation is required to be assertive and follow through on what it is you truly desire. The markers that help you identify when something needs to shift, change, or be released can show up in many ways. It can show up in our body, our emotions, who we surround ourselves with, and what we choose to avoid.

For me, my body tells me when I am in moments of distress. My mind, however, for many years, had been disconnected from my body. In the past, I would get to moments of true physical break-down before I had a wakeup call to break through bad habits, choices, and patterns I thought I had to follow to be successful. I thought I had to comply with what others thought I should be or do, in order to receive love. In turn, it resulted with a broken life. I was not always in a positive mindset that I deserved the best; my self-worth was low and at times I was self-destructive.

Self-destructive behavior comes from emotional imbalance and for me, it was a lack of self-worth and self-love that would result in physical dysfunction. This mindset was developed at a young age when I didn't really know I had a choice on what to believe about myself. I just believed what was repeatedly said, a certain look, a rejection, and that I had the inability to be heard. What I didn't realize is that I was being raised by the limitations of others. It was not my parents' fault that they did not know how to love me the way I needed; they tried their best. And when they went through the trauma of divorce, I was in my most impressionable years when it came to my femininity and forming my own thoughts about myself. I was at the awkward stage of 11 when it all started and did not find a safe space to share my emotions until I was 16.

My self-destructive behaviors would show up in overeating and extending myself at school and side jobs so I could avoid home. One time I was in so much emotional pain and anger and didn't have an outlet, that I decided to ram my elbow bare skinned down the brick wall of our school stairs just to feel something. At that time, I had learned to keep up appearances and still get my home-work done, was the president of my class, and was on varsity sports teams. I had learned that regardless of how I am really feeling, it was more important that I appeared ok to others. There was a lot for me to unlearn in years to come.

I had created a self-loathing, all-accepting mindset.

I would empathize with anyone in pain with ease because I com-pletely understood it; I was in pain too. My overachiever side had a story that if I could help them feel less pain, at least I was doing something good. This attracted situations in my life that I probably could have avoided, but every person I attracted was a reflection of how I truly felt about myself.

The worst case of this self-loathing, all-accepting mindset was when I was 23, in my first job out of college, living on my own in that studio apartment I was so proud of living in. As much as get-ting that apartment was a triumphant moment, my life choices at the time were not. The first temp job I had at the art school, where I only worked for about ten weeks, had hired ex-convicts to drive their shuttle buses throughout the city to get the college kids to their classes on time. These men were part of the Delancey Street program that helped them rehabilitate into real life. The operations department I was working with managed this group of men and their schedules. It was a great program, however, I did not realize these men were ex-cons until weeks after I had started the job and befriended them. I was new to town and really wanted to make new friends, so I was open to everyone. I allowed one of the bus drivers to drop me off at home one night because it was late and he offered. My commute was not that far, but it was easier than waiting for the bus. We joked and laughed as we got to know each other. I had no idea about his past until after he knew where I lived.

He became way too attached to my kindness and was obsessed with trying to make me his girlfriend. You would think after my exposure to living in Washington, DC and many visits to Manhattan, I would have known how to protect myself from this situation. I was so naïve. Other than my cousin, I really did not have many friends at this point in San Francisco. I was thankful I had my neighbor downstairs if I needed to call in an emergency. I really felt alone and afraid. I didn't know what to do. He would show up at my apartment unannounced and somehow get into my apartment building and start knocking on the door to see if I was there. I would sit quietly and hope that if I pretended not to be there, he would leave. He eventually would give up and leave. I sat in my apartment crying with a knife in my hand just in case he would break in. I would leave it by my bed at night to try and sleep. I was freaked out, but I kept all of this to myself.

I didn't want to call the police and put him back in jail, which is what my now Badass-self would have done for harassing me. I didn't want his life to have any more pain. I feared doing that on my own, and the potential repercussions. I never told my family this story because they were living in other states, so what could they do? Plus, I was ashamed that I let this man into my life. I also needed the job to pay my bills and didn't want to risk losing it. I figured if I could just get another job and get away from him, the distance would calm his obsession with me. Nothing good comes from living out of fear, but that is what I had to do to survive.

• • • • • •

I eventually got another job, and would repeatedly tell him to leave me alone when he called. He finally did. I am grateful nothing happened to me physically, but emotionally I had masked my fear with distance and focused on achievement so I could work my way out of that life. I knew that if I continued to make more money, I could provide a life for myself where I would not compromise like that again and let people into my life that were not worthy of my time.

It took me many years before I realized my worth and built reciprocal relationships vs. the ones I created based on fear and feeling lonely. The men I attracted into my life, my bed, and my heart at that time were all broken and lost. I just wanted to feel wanted. They reflected how disconnected I really was from my heart and my body. I never had healthy body image of myself. When attractive men would show their attraction to me, I would not believe it.

During the first few years in San Francisco, I could not afford healthy, organic, clean food and honestly, it would not help me manage my stress to eat that way. I wanted McDonald's, and large, cheap burritos. I wanted large alcoholic beverages and a pack of cigarettes to calm my pain. These were habits I had learned in college to self-soothe. I was so disconnected with my body that my actions made me numb it even further. The crazy part was I was highly functional in my job. My stress levels were through the roof, I am sure my blood pressure was way off too, but I never went in for physicals. My daily regimen of lunch at McDonald's and "super sizing" everything was not the cleanest way to live...and it was catching up with me.

Luckily, this was around the time my bestie from college moved to San Francisco. She kept telling me I was not the Kareen she knew. She cared for me so much and was observing my behavior—how I looked, and how disconnected I was from my actions—and she would say: "Quit your f'ing job, Kareen," before I left for work each day. She could see how the stress was slowly killing me. I would hear her words but I was so numb from layering on emotional fat to protect me from feeling my pain and sadness, that I ignored her until I had a health scare.

● ● ● ● ● ●

One night, which is now known as the "WWF Night" (WWF stands for Worldwide Wrestling Federation, for those of you who may not have watched wrestling in the 80's/90's), I had severe cramping in my abdominal region. I remember it feeling like someone had tied up all my stomach muscles and pulled tight to connect them together. I could barely move but knew I had to get to the bathroom in case I was going to have a surge in my system to release whatever it was.

I lifted my head, moaned in pain and told my bestie that I was not feeling good and headed to the bathroom.

"I feel like I might pass out," I said, and was a bit dizzy. The bathroom was only ten steps away but it felt like miles. I managed to get on the toilet just in case I needed to release whatever was going on, and instead, I could feel myself passing out. My vision got dark and I started to tilt forward, moaning: "I am about to pass out; get something that has a scent to it, and wave it under my nose to help me come to." My head fell between my knees and I was out. She did as I suggested and I came to. I was still sitting on the toilet and leaning on the side wall to get my bearings.

"Come on, let me get you back to bed," she said and got me to stand up and lean on her as we made our way into the hallway. I passed out again leaning against the wall. She put her arms under my armpits to help me stay standing and walk to the bed. I fell to my knees. I was in and out of consciousness over the small distance three times. She finally got me to the edge of my bed. I could see it. She released her arms to allow me to fall into bed....

Instead, I pivoted left and WWF'ed my nightstand.

I hit my face on the lamp, then the nightstand, and ended up passed out on the floor. I came to again for a few minutes, realized I was on the ground and asked, "Why does my face hurt?"

"I don't know what the F is wrong with you, but I am calling 911."

"Ok," I said, and passed out again.

Prior to the fire department and paramedics showing up, I came to. I was more lucid this time. The cramping was still there, but I could articulate my thoughts. I was sitting and leaning against the bed and my friend's eyes were so wide and full of fear. She was freaking out. I assured her I would be ok. I had no idea what was happening to me, but I didn't want her to feel my fear. Then, all these men started to pile into my small studio apartment: four firemen and two paramedics. The paramedics took my vitals and said I seemed fine, but recommended I go to the ER to get more tests done just in case. I agreed and my bestie came with me.

We got to the ER and they put me in a room that looked like a closet for crutches. I remember passing the nurses station and really feeling like they could give a shit why I was there and I was so thankful my friend was along to help me. I went into the bathroom and it felt like my body exploded. I finally released whatever was taking over. After heading back to the room they had me in, I felt ten times better.

A doctor finally came in to check on me, and said, "Everything is fine based on your tests. Just ice your head and lip and keep taking the medication you are on. Go check in with your primary doctor later today." What a waste of time. We called a cab and headed home. That incident was the start of my assessment of "what the heck I was doing with my life...and for what?"

I share this story with you because I want to illustrate the importance of looking at your life as a whole. All areas of our life matter in order to make up a fulfilled Badass Life!

● ● ● ● ● ●

In that phase of my life, I was so focused on my work and earning a check because I didn't want to fail people's expectations of me or return home, that I sacrificed my health to manage the stress I was under. I was in the ER after I WWF'ed my nightstand and stressed about what I was going to do about work, getting there on time, and following through on being responsible for other people's needs before my own. My foundation was built on sand. I did not have a concept of self-care at the time. I was in Survival Mode...and I was miserable.

The next day, I had walked into the office with a new lens. At the time, I had just received notice that the VP I was working for decided to hire a director that I would be reporting to. I remember thinking how awesome it would be to have someone show me the ropes and guide my growth in the company. And maybe, just maybe, I could unload some of the work onto someone else so I could find some time to care for myself. All of a sudden, I was on around-the-clock support and there were no boundaries; my pager was never off. Lack of sleep, poor eating habits, and high-stress as an entry level person on the job...no wonder I was having health issues! When I heard they were bringing in someone new for me to report to, I had such high hopes for her arrival. This was the change I needed to get things back on track. I was mistaken.

Imagine being age 23 and hitting a glass ceiling. I had been on the job for about eight months. My new manager had started and she was a fierce woman. I was so excited to have someone with experience to teach me how to build my career and grow within my role. However, this woman had a different agenda. What I had not realized at the time was that she was threatened by me.

The support team I was on had gotten accustomed to coming to me for advice, process layout, and task distribution. Every time she met with other team members asking about what they do and how they do it, all roads led back to me as the "manager" of it all. I was just doing what I thought would be best for the team and our internal clients. I was front-line support, so I would get all the requests and distribute them out. I also was responsible for business resumption if we had system errors occur that would stop their daily operations and would be the one to escalate to the team to resolve the issues. It was way more than I was hired to do, but it needed to be done.

I was finally at a point in my time at the job where I needed to know what direction it was headed. I had scheduled a 1:1 with my new boss to help her understand my role on the team and ask for guidance about what was next. I remember putting together a two-column list where on the left side of the paper was the job I was hired for about eight months back, and the actual role I was playing was listed out on the right side of the paper. I wanted to illustrate the responsibility and increase in duties so that she would have full knowledge of what I was doing, and to help me understand if I had a growth plan on the team. We were in a four-person conference room and I was prepping myself for the meeting by taking deep breaths and saying to myself, "Kareen, you have nothing to lose. Share with her where you are, and I am sure she will guide you with next steps."

We started the meeting, and I realized she never smiled when she looked at me. I think she was trained with intimidation tactics when she was in the army twenty years prior. I first started with thanking her for meeting with me to discuss my current role and to help me understand if there was a role I could grow into on the team. I shared my document with her and walked her through the activities. Then I asked what she thought and if she saw a growth plan for me.

I will never forget the reaction. With a smirk on her face she said, "Kareen, I don't know what you are complaining about, what you are doing is your job, just keep doing it." Then, she ended the meeting and that was that. No mention of how long I would need to do this job to grow into something else, no thoughts of consideration on how to help me increase my skill set so I could earn more and grow within the company. Nothing.

I felt so deflated after the conversation. What was I doing so much for? Why was I stretching myself so much for a job and a manager that was not going to help me get to the next level in my career? I was so overwhelmed with emotion. I remember being thankful it was a Thursday so I would only have to show up on Friday and have the weekend to decide what to do next. I was in shock. I took the weekend to assess the pro's and con's of staying in the job. I mustered up the courage to talk to my mom about it all.

My mom is someone who never lets anyone dictate how her life could be, and she taught us to do the same. I recounted the conversation with my boss to my mom, crying, not sure what to do next. I didn't have the fight in me anymore to sustain the stressful situation. She then said, "Kareen, I think you should quit the job and find something else. You did not come this far to suffer under someone else's limitations. I support whatever you decide."

Relief came over me. I had an option, a safety net if I needed it, and the support of my mother to do something for myself that was risky but worth it for my overall health. I was paralyzed for a bit trying to figure out if it was really true. Once it set in, I knew what I had to do next: resign. I went into the office on Monday morning and sent my resignation email to my boss. I gave her two weeks and I was out.

I knew I made the right decision, as scary as it was. Then, I found out that I was replaced by a man, whose base salary was $60,000—$22,000 more than what I was earning. He also got to hire an assistant at $45,000 to do all the work that I had done for the team! All I was looking for was a growth plan and ability to earn more. I was making $38,000 at the time and had been replaced by two men for a cost to the company of $105,000 just because the manager was threatened by me and wanted someone in the role she could control with ease. It was the best lesson for me to have so early on in my career because it taught me three things:

1. *I learned that people lead through their own limitations, and their limitations are not for me to carry or represent what I am capable of earning.*

2. *Always ask for what you think you deserve. If the answer is no, then it is your choice to embrace the no and decide what is right for you.*

3. *Taking a risk to go after what you really want and learning from your mistakes is living life.*

It was a Bold and Assertive move to take my life into my own hands again. I was thoughtful and methodical about taking the risk to leave the job and would not have found the company or opportunity to grow that led to the Badass Moment on Chestnut Street only four years later.

● ● ● ● ● ●

It took me years to unravel the damage I had done in my 20's and wanted to learn how to master my health so I could show up in my life as the Badass I knew I was in all areas. I had mastered the art of making money and taking risks to achieve, but I failed miserably when it came to self-care. I had started to rely on holistic practices to break my bad habits and leveraged the expertise of others to help me heal. I wanted to help others do the same, so I decided to dive in and study nutrition and holistic health.

I want to share with you an assessment tool that I learned in my 30's when I studied to be a Certified Holistic Health Coach through the Institute of Integrative Nutrition in 2010. I wish I had this tool in my 20's to help me clearly identify areas of my life that needed a boost. This is a visual exercise to help you assess where you stand in certain areas of your life. Try it and be honest; it is the only way for you to identify what is holding you back from your Badass Life. I promise if you stick with the exercises to follow, you will have a map that gets you from a Lame-ass life to a Badass one, in no time.

Tool #2: Assess Where You Are
Today: Circle of Life Exercise

Now that you have some clarity on your Vision Life, let's assess how you think things are going today. This is a simple exercise where you plot the dots of where you rate your life today in the slice of the circle that represents an area of life. The outer rim of the circle represents pure satisfaction/fulfillment; nothing needs to change, everything is amazing! If it is a 10 out of 10 fulfillment in that area, the dot should be placed on the outer rim of the circle in that arena. The center point represents dissatisfaction.

A. First, plot your dots in each relevant slice of the circle on how fulfilled you are today, then connect them.

B. Second, plot your Vision Life on the Circle of Life.

On the same Circle of Life image, I want you to visualize your Vision Life and then plot the dot where you think it best represents your Vision Life. Then connect them. Try to use a different color pen or marker so you can see the difference from where you are today, and where you plan to be.

C. Now, write down what the differences are. Are the results that represent today close to your desired Vision Life? Are they far off? What did you discover?

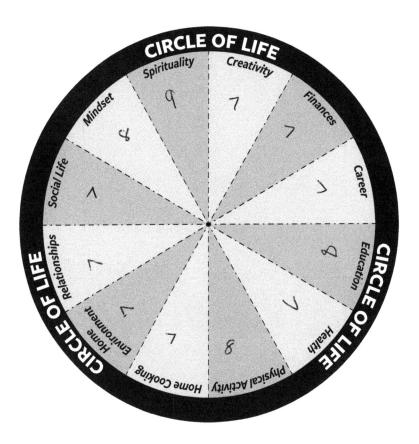

To download the workbook associated with this book, visit
www.kareenwalsh.com/beabadass.

CHAPTER 3

I AM DRIVEN.

The things that drive us, move us forward. When you align your activities with your desired goals, you get closer to your Vision Life. When you are in doubt, get distracted, or feel unsure, I want you to repeat this mantra: **I am Driven**. When repeated, this mantra will become a habit towards getting clarity on what you want to create in your life. Give yourself some grace through the learning process, and once you are clear, get into action.

A Badass Sets Goals in Order to Achieve Anything in Life

The number one excuse I hear when someone wants to see a shift in their life is that they don't have enough time! We all have the same hours in a day; how we choose to use them is what creates a Badass Life!

Each morning, we have a choice on how we want to spend our day, where we want to invest in ourselves, and who we choose to show up for. I did not have healthy daily habits for a long time. I planned how I spent my time based on the demands of others first, then would try to squeeze in some "me time" on occasion. When it was not consistent, the dysfunctional cycle I was living continued day in and day out. I had to choose to break the cycle and build Badass Daily Habits that fuel my Vision Life each day.

In the previous chapter, I shared how bad my health had gotten and how I was so disconnected from my body. For me, it was way easier to jump into my intellect and succeed in my overachiever life because I learned this skill at a young age. My default was to ignore my true emotions, judge myself to believe I was not physically capable of pushing myself in sports, or did not look good enough to attract a handsome, healthy, successful man, and I would fall into the background to help others shine. Even my intellect would get challenged while growing up in private school. From first through eighth grade I was placed in special reading and writing tutoring groups.

I started to rely on my gifts of building relationships and taking care of others just to find a form of appreciation and accolades for who I was. It 100% impacted how I chose to spend my time through my 20's and completely shifted when I entered my 30's started to put me first. I discovered methods of self-care and actually built the time into my schedule to unravel bad habits and replace them with more fulfilling activities.

Now that you have gone through the Circle of Life exercise and compared where you are today to where you want to be, there are gaps, right? I would like you to pick an area in your life to focus on improving—I would suggest one that has the largest gap of satisfaction/fulfillment levels. A Badass Move is to face the area of your life that is not satisfactory and then commit to up-leveling yourself as you continue to go through this book. Outline the goals or statements that represent the Vision Life you have for yourself in this area. It could be any area outlined: Relationships, Career, Finances, Spirituality, Health, Social Life, Home Environment, Adventure, etc.

Once you have picked the area you want to focus on, I would like you to write down what you plan to be.

An example:

I plan to be a best-selling author so I can extend my reach and impact more lives. Because of my publications, I will be asked to do keynote speeches and book signings. I will meet my audience face-to-face to understand how their lives have been impacted and what else I can assist them with.

● ● ● ● ● ●

There are so many versions of us, especially as a Badass, because we are not just one thing. Add adjectives and characteristics to really make it unique to your life, your path, and your vision. Take five minutes, and write out some solid statements that are true to you. (Remember, we are not here to judge, we are here to get the truth out and be real with ourselves.) Then, write an example of a goal that you would like to achieve as part of your Vision Life now, so you can get it down and you can use it as a thread in the exercises to come.

When you have clarity on what would fill you up in this area, it will help you identify activities that need to change and where to spend your time to add in the new habits that help you get closer to your goal. In this case, your goal is a higher level of satisfaction in an area that is underserved and holding you back from your Badass Life.

● ● ● ● ● ●

After making the decision to resign from the job that allowed me to have the Badass Moment on Chestnut Street, I moved to Colorado with new intentions on how I wanted my life to be. I had envisioned living a healthy life at a slower pace. I envisioned making sure my income earning methods would be able to afford the healthy life-style choices I wanted but not put me back into a stress cycle I could not control. Based on my skillset and achievements in my career, I had certainty that I would find work; however, I was not sure I wanted to stay in the industry I was in, so I was also open to new opportunities.

Buying my first house in Denver was another Badass Moment. I managed to secure the home purchase prior to resigning, so all my paperwork and approvals were in order. I remember the pride I had in what my income and credit score could afford me, and the money I had saved for the down payment to purchase my first home on my own. In less than six years, I went from paying for a studio apartment at $495/month to purchasing my first home for $207,000. My mortgage payments were about $1,300/month, which was perfect. I remember thinking if I only earned $50,000 a year, I could still afford that house and have a great life in Denver. I knew I would earn more, so the additional earnings would go into investing into my health, and making sure the time I spent daily was focused on that. I was fortunate that when I resigned from my job, they asked me to stay longer to manage the transition to another manager and make sure all I had built for the company was managed with ease upon my departure. I, of course, said yes, and negotiated a deal where they would pay me a bonus on top of my salary to stay two months longer and pay for my travel back and forth to Denver. *Damn, I was such a bold Badass back then!*

I had learned how the system worked and how they would treat valued employees, so I made sure I asked for what I deserved. I had nothing to lose! I already set myself up in Denver, and it was all a matter of timing before I would start my life there full time. I didn't have a job yet, so there was no rush to leave. I transitioned my responsibilities to the manager I had groomed, and repainted and furnished my home in Denver on my trips back and forth. So, when it came time to move to Denver full time, I was all set up.

My social circle at the time was mainly in the restaurant industry, since I could not socialize that much with my former co-workers, so I would sit at the bars of restaurants or go to sushi bars to be able to talk and interact with people while eating. I ended up befriending a lot of people in the industry and also got a lot of food and drinks for free along the way, which was nice. I did not have a network of professionals in my field, so I basically had to start over.

I realized that for my skill set and the level I had built up in a financial services software company, the opportunities for me were slim and lower pay than I anticipated as a full-time employee. That was when I learned about how to be self-employed and work from contract to contract, making just as much income with way more flexibility.

I said yes to a subcontract for a position I was completely over-qualified for, but the income was the same as what I was making in San Francisco, and I didn't have to work as hard. I developed a philosophy of *Minimal Effort/Maximum Reward* when it came to my work life. The income and flexibility in my schedule allowed me to focus on my health and my mindset and really get clear on what I wanted to achieve. That's how I came up with the method below that I want to share with you.

Tool #3: What Fills You Up? Assessing Your Fulfillment Factor

This exercise gives you the ability to assess where you are spending your time today, review how fulfilling it is, and what you might need to add in or let go to take-action towards your Vision Life in the arena you have selected to focus on. I recommend you go through this exercise focused on that arena: Health, Finances, Career, Family Life, Fitness Level, Spirituality, Creativity, etc.

Some of us have been trained on how to get things done for other people with ease, whether it is through work or home life. When given a task, we can list them and cross them off our list.

A task list with no purpose affects our levels of satisfaction and fulfillment in how we spend our time. Now that you have an idea of where you want to go, we need to figure out how to move in the right direction. How do we leverage what we want and how to get there with ease? (I recommend you download the workbook to centralize your answers in one place; it gives you more room to write everything out.)

1. Pick a goal or statement from work above that you would like to achieve in the next 90 days. Write it down.

2. In this space, assess what skills you already HAVE, what resources or qualifications are already in your life that you can leverage to obtain this goal, and write them down. Then write down if you need to acquire any new skills to obtain this goal. If you can think of any additional steps you need to take to obtain this goal, list them out.

3. Time to prioritize and map out actions to achieve your goal. Now that you have your goal and the tasks to achieve it listed out, place a prioritization number or order of operation of what should happen first before you move to the next item on the list to achieve the goal. Simply put a number next to the top three things that, you were to do first, would get you closer to your goal. Write down the top three actions.

4. BAM! You have a plan of action to achieve that one goal! Taking action towards your Vision Life does not need a laundry list of items to fulfill. Start with your top three and you will start moving towards your goals with ease and eliminate overwhelm. When those items are mastered, pick up the next three priorities. You can do this exercise repeatedly in all areas of your life!

Now when you look at the Vision Life goal, and how you broke down a few actions to take to help you inch towards it, I want you to visualize what it will feel like when you achieve it.

Do you have a sense of pride and joy?

Does this new version of you feel fulfilled by achieving this goal?

What you spend your time on directly impacts how fulfilling your life is!

Where are you spending your time? Now we have to figure out where we fit these actions into your daily routine. In order to do this, we need to assess the level of fulfillment of where you spend your time today!

A. List out where you spend time today

Grab a few pieces of paper and put "Be a Badass" at the top. I want you to write out all the ACTIVITIES you do daily across all arenas of your life. Ignore the FF and Action Columns for now.

Just make your list of activities and where you spend your time. Header:

ACTIVITY	FF NOW	FF VL	ACTION

B. Score the level of fulfillment against each activity

Put a number from 1-10 (1 being feel nothing, 10 being totally ful-filled and excited) in Column FF NOW—I want you to rate how fulfilling this activity is for your life today. Go through the whole list of activities before you do the next step.

C. Score the level of fulfillment against each activity as if you were living your Vision Life

Now think about your Vision Life, the life you know that if you lived, it would feel amazing and aligned with where you are meant to be. Put a number from 1-10 (1 being feel nothing, 10 being totally fulfilled and excited) in Column FF VL.

You should put low scores of the activities that don't bring you fulfillment in your Vision Life if you continue to do them.

I want you to rate how fulfilling each activity is for your life today. Go through the whole list of activities before you do the next step.

D. Imagine and list the daily activities in your Vision Life

Take a moment and list out the daily activities you visualize doing in your Vision Life. What would you do first thing in the morning? What would you do with your afternoons? How would you spend your nights if you have reached the life you plan to achieve and dream of? What are those activities? List them out.

E. Grouping

Take the list of activities that have a score of 8 or above for both FF NOW and FF VL from your first sheet and list them together.

Next, take the list of the activities that have a score of 6 or less for FF NOW and FF VL and list them together.

F. Weed whacking

Now it's time to take action. You listed activities that would help you achieve your Vision Life against the goal you choose. Looking at the list for activities that have a score less than 7; what can you do to remove them from your list of activities? Can you delegate them, ask for help, or let them go?

Use the following codes to help you organize what actions you need to take to remove the less fulfilling activities from your life. (Delegate = D, H = Help, Let it Go = L) You can use whatever codes you want to help you identify what action you will take to raise your fulfillment levels.

G. Increasing fulfilling activities

Review your list of 8 or above from the activities you do today, and the list of activities you envision to build your Vision Life. Pick three activities you would like to start doing more of, or add in, from your Vision Life list. Write them down.

Be selective. Choose the top three with the highest fulfillment factor. We want to focus on what fills you up.

Here are some great self-assessment questions when you feel stuck between now and what you want to achieve. Getting real with ourselves is the best way to ensure we are taking an actionable step towards what we truly want to add to our lives and what we want to let go.

1. **Take Inventory:** What do I have that already qualifies me to achieve this goal?

2. **Needs Assessment:** What do I need to achieve this goal?

3. **Purge:** What do I need to let go of, or remove from my life in order to achieve this goal?

Repeat your mantra to help you let go of what no longer serves you and add in new activities to align who you are with the life you want to lead. Letting go can be uncomfortable sometimes; find gratitude in each lesson and move forward. You've got this!

CHAPTER 4

I AM ALIGNED.

Imagine, doing all this work to identify what it is that you want, and not realizing there was so much that you needed to let go of in order to create the space for the life you dream of. It can be an anxiety-ridden response when you realize you are in a life that you chose and see that so much of it is unfulfilling. That was me.

Yes, I had a life where I could afford more than most and go on amazing adventures and take risks, but like I have said before, I was miserable inside. *I got so used to my discomfort that it became my comfort zone.* I started to attract the pain I was carrying around in the people I surrounded myself with. I did not feel like a Badass. I knew that I deserved best life. Why was I making so many decisions that did not represent the Vision Life I wanted for myself?

The seeker in me wanted to find the way to do it. As I mentioned before, I was highly functional in my dysfunction, which started in my younger years, and I was not able to unravel and mend until I learned the power of forgiveness. Before I get to that magical lesson that has forever changed my life, I need to bring you into my darkness because I want to make sure you understand how this deeply-rooted, destructive self-belief dictated the poor choices in my life.

● ● ● ● ● ●

I was emotionally bankrupt when it came to navigating an intimate relationship. I wanted to be married but had no clue what a real marriage looked like because my parents officially divorced when I was around age 13, and my role in the family shifted from child to parent in a matter of minutes. I imagined an amazing wedding to the man of my dreams, having two to four kids, living in a gorgeous house, and having the means to raise them and work at the same time. It was an amazing fairy tale dream, with really no foundation on understanding what it was like to sustain and create a healthy relationship.

In my college years, I learned I was attractive, and guys were into me. I had a college boyfriend that adored me and cared for me, but he did not meet my mother's standards. She made me feel like shit for loving him because she feared that he did not represent the life I deserved. In her upbringing, dating meant engaged. It was a very confusing time for me, because it was the first time I had received unconditional love from someone that was not family, and I was being alienated as a result. I was still in the mindset that I had to have my mother's approval on my choices, so when she did not approve, I subconsciously questioned my love for the man in my life. Years later, I almost married a man that was so wrong for me in so many ways due to what I believed about myself at the time.

- I believed that no man could ever hurt me like my father did (this story was created by the distance he created when my parents got divorced and he left the country to pursue his own life).
- The other story was that I was not worthy of receiving the love I gave because I would never be good enough (my mother's love lesson).

If you were to have this mindset trying to be in a relationship with another person, what type of person do you think you would attract?

● ● ● ● ● ●

I had mended my relationship with my father the best I could, when I was a junior in college. I decided to spend the summer with him and his girlfriend in Switzerland before my senior year. He moved to Switzerland after he had lost his business when I was 16 and had to declare personal and corporate bankruptcy. I have blackout periods in my memory of that time due to emotional trauma and high-stress levels where I don't remember what I did, I was just going through the motions and trying to survive. My dad had been through a lot, was not in his right mind, and would say things to me that I thought were unacceptable. So, I created distance and told him not to be in touch with me between the ages of 16-18. Deciding to spend the time with him in Switzerland was a big deal.

My relationship with my boyfriend at the time awakened me to unconditional love. I wanted to mend my relationship with my father and not hurt anymore from our relationship. I realized during that stay that he never had the skill to parent his children. It was not a desire of his. His primary focus was success and his lack of emotional connection was not mine to carry. I saw him for who he is and what he is capable of, and as his daughter his level of emotional support and inability to protect me as his daughter, just wasn't enough.

During that trip, I voiced my pains to him. He listened. He cried with me. He apologized. He asked for forgiveness. I forgave him and let go of any expectations I had. You would think this would release me of some of my dysfunction towards my relationship with men. It didn't. Because I didn't learn my beliefs about love from my father, I learned them from my mother. However, I did not realize this until nine years later, only four months before I was about to walk down the aisle and marry the wrong man for me.

I respect and love my mother dearly and she has taught me the best lessons. We are a lot alike in our emotional makeup. I craved her love so much as a child and when it was met with conditions, I never felt good enough. It was not her intention for me to feel that way; it was the skill she had at the time and what she was capable of giving under the circumstances. I know 100% she only wants the best for me, and will probably be the first person to buy my book and support my goals.

What I appreciate most about my mom is that she is willing to have a conversation now and grow with me. I have advised her several times over different areas in her life that she asked for help with, and I appreciate her confidence in me to assist her. There was a time, however, where she did take advantage of my giving nature as a child, which conditioned me and my mindset to accept people in my life that were not worthy of my time. I had not learned how to create the healthy boundaries needed to maintain a healthy relationship.

These were lessons I had to unlearn and reconnect with myself to know truly what I wanted, what I needed to let go of, and what boundaries I had to set to make sure she and I could build a foundation that worked for both of us. These experiences are something that truly shifted my way of being.

● ● ● ● ● ●

My courage to face the discomfort and the cycle of self-sabotage allowed me to see the other side of the emotional cycles that hinder personal growth. When I was engaged the first time, I was going to therapy to work through my bouts with depression and cyclical desire to inflict pain on myself after certain conversations with my mother. In those sessions, the root of the problem came from never being able to please her. I also uncovered that the way she was speaking to me, demanding of me, and treating me was emotionally abusive. It was her way or no way. I reacted to our conversations with inner anger and hurt, which would result in self-sabotage. I would overeat and allow wrong people into my life that offered only unhealthy love in return for the love I gave. My bar was set so low I welcomed in others who were in pain because I could relate. I also thought if I could relieve their pain a bit, then I was at least helping someone else get the relief I desired.

It was not easy to face my emotional imbalance with my mother because it was so deeply rooted from my childhood. I was an obedient child and wanted to please her, and the middle child in me just wanted to matter. I am a responsible, loving person and able take on a lot because I was asked to while I was still young. I built up a resilience that blocked my true emotions and just plowed through hard things to get them done. I was 32. I realized that I did not want a future with burdensome thoughts and self-sabotaging actions every time I was on the receiving end of my mom's emotions. When was it my turn? When was I going to be loved and nurtured in a way she received from me? When was my voice going to matter? When would the cycle stop?

● ● ● ● ● ●

Well, it all starts and stops with me, right? So, I had to be brave and face it. The most vivid memory I had about the verbal abuse and overextended requirements of my role in the family was after my older sister got married. That year was when I started to put distance between my mother and me so I could figure out my emotions and build the stance in our relationship that worked for me. I was burned out from always catering to our mom's needs and being her confidante when it did not serve me. I just wanted a fun celebratory weekend with my sister without all the heaviness. It was hard for me, but my sister was gracious enough to keep checking on me and making sure that I was ok. She is so protective of me at times and understands my pain.

Going through the process of identifying what was not right in my relationship with my mom was not easy and probably the hardest emotional work I have ever done. When my sister would validate the emotional abuse for me through her observations, it would strengthen my desire to work through it and change the foundation of my relationship with my mom. About a week after the wedding, my mom called to unleash her feelings on me. I was in shock for most of it and did a lot of self-talk that sounded a bit like:

"This is emotional abuse and what she is demanding of you is not acceptable of a mother to a daughter. You are not responsible for how she relates to others in the family. You are not her spouse. You are not her companion. You are not her emotional punching bag. You are her daughter and deserve to be loved and adored and taken care of. You deserve to be protected and nurtured. This right here, this is unacceptable."

• • • • • •

I was sitting on my couch with my knees to my chest, phone to ear, and her going off on me with statements like, "How could you," and "You should have," and all sorts of comments on how it was my fault that she was not included the way she saw fit and how excluding her was unacceptable. She called me selfish, mean, inconsiderate, and many other things that she probably doesn't remember because she was hurt. And when she was hurt, she was used to confiding in me and unleashing all of her pain onto me to hold. In the past, I would listen, console her, try to fix it, because it was a role I was put in at a young age and I didn't know any better. I let her vent because I knew it would be the last time she would cross this boundary with me.

I was dead silent on the other end not responding, until she finally took a breath and said, "Kareen, are you still there?"

"Mom, I can't do this anymore," I answered, crying. "I am not responsible for the relationship you have with my sisters or anyone else for that matter. I am not responsible for making sure you fit in when you have created a space of tension that is not my doing. I am no longer going to be your emotional punching bag when you are having down days. I need to focus on me and what I want and I think it is best we have distance between us for a while. I am sorry you are hurting, and it did not happen the way you wanted, but that is not for me to fix either. Please don't call me for a while, I need space to work things out for myself. What I know for sure, is our relationship cannot continue like this." I was shaking as I spoke.

I had done the work to get the words out, but it still hurt to put them out there and it was scary because I did not know how she would respond. But, I had to care for myself first. It was so worth it.

This was the beginning of our relationship rebirth. I had to think of my needs before hers and stand by them. Distance and time were the two best things to work through it all. I continued with therapy to work through what I wanted and how I envisioned the relationship could be. My mom and I had a deep love for each other, but we just did not have the right boundaries for both of us to be our best when together. We had to shift it and it all started with me to determine who I let into my life and how I wanted the relationship to work for me. If it wasn't a fit, I needed to let it go. Even if it was a family member. What I knew for sure is I wanted a relationship with her, just not the one we had.

That release of an unfulfilling relationship and build-up of self-love is what brought me to realize that my fiancé was not right for me. He had his own baggage and ways of living that did not represent my best self. It reflected in the level of conditional love I accepted from my mother, which was met with pain and hurt most of the time. I knew I deserved more, and he was not at a point where he was interested in growing with me. Deciding to move on was the best thing for both of us.

And, you will never imagine what I did next: I went to go live with my mother for six months and work on our relationship! Can you believe it? I knew that if I did not spend time with my mother face to face, I could not heal in a way to bring the love into my life that I deserve.

First, there must be self-love, which can't be true until you face the negative thoughts that keep you away from the purest love you have for yourself.

Second, there must be true love for another, which is never true if you don't love yourself first.

● ● ● ● ● ●

Before I move into sharing how I created the opportunity to go live with my mother after ending my engagement, I want to pause and give you the opportunity to leverage the work you have already done in Chapter 3 of this book.

You are Driven because you can focus on tasks at hand. In Chapter 3 of this book, we discussed your fulfillment factor and rated what fills you up. The reason I share this self-worth and self-love story with you about my relationship with my mother is to show you that even as an over-achiever, accomplishing everything on my list and finding "success," I was not aligned on the inside. I did not have the capacity to enjoy my wins because my mindset focused on the 3% missing when I would get a 97% out of 100%. I was taught to focus on that 3% and strive for more. It was not fulfilling. I had to get to the root of why. And when the root is an emotional one, I had to shift the energy and design the relationship I required to fill me up.

● ● ● ● ● ●

I want you to take a moment and look at the list of items you did in your fulfillment factor that have a score of less than 5. I would like you to ask yourself the following when you look at that list:

How does this activity make me feel? Who am I doing the task for? Why do I feel obligated to do it?

If a person comes to mind that triggers any negative emotion around that low fulfillment score item, write their name next to it.

Then ask yourself, "If my relationship was different with this person, would the task be more fulfilling?"

I ask you this because it took me a long time to realize the undertone of my discomfort. It took a long time for me to do the work and discover that the dysfunctional root in my emotional story created a misalignment in other areas of my life that I did not realize. Talk therapy comes in handy when it is a relationship or deep-rooted emotional story that stops you from living a fulfilled life. Seek out a professional to work with if you need to find the tools to break the cycle and rewire the relationship with this person. It was the best work I have ever done. The tools I now use to sustain my alignment in self-love and self-worth come next.

• • • • • •

Since I was an independent consultant at the time working for myself, I could really work anywhere. I had gone to Washington, DC for a week for a certification course I wanted to take to increase my credentials and stayed with my mom. By this time, we had mended a lot of our differences over the phone and at a distance. She was there for me when I shared that I ended the engagement and canceled the wedding. She was proud of me for not compromising and ending it now before it could lead to a divorce later.

During that time in DC, I met a woman in my class that said she would love to have me come work with her. I was excited because I needed a change of scenery from Denver. I was going back and forth on working with this woman, and it ultimately fell through. However, I still wanted to follow through with my plan to get away for six months and be in the DC area, so I reached out to my friends to see if they knew of anyone looking for my skillset. I managed to network my way into a contract gig with AOL, which was in Dulles, Virginia. Perfect! I rented my house in Denver, packed a few bags, and moved into my mom's garden level apartment and worked at AOL.

My mom and I had a weekly dinner to connect and talk through our relationship. I could share what did not serve me well. She did her best to listen and asked for forgiveness. This was a huge turning point for me because I found strength in my voice, my desires, and my self-love became so much stronger. I also could trust that regardless of how my mother would react to what I was saying, my emotions mattered, and it was up to me to express them without any expectation of a reaction and allow her to have the reaction she needed. It was a lesson learned that has affected all my relationships since. I learned to:

1. *Meet people where they are.*

2. *Be myself.*

3. *When it hurts, express it.*

4. *Forgive others to see things for what they are today, not the past.*

● ● ● ● ● ●

After my six-month stint in DC, I decided to go spend two weeks with my aunt in Dubai. Earlier that year, my cousin (her son), died in a motorcycle accident. This was the cousin I lived with in San Francisco and celebrated the 2005 New Year in Dubai. He was the male version of me and I miss him dearly. I knew that he would want me to spend more time with his mom and help her heal, so I did to honor my love for him.

This was a hard time for her, but she would find the energy each day to get up, pray, and cry as she helped others with whatever they needed. She lived on the second floor flat of a three-story building in one of the pre-fabricated home communities outside of the city of Dubai. It was on a man-made lake and resembled California homes in its construct. If you have never been to Dubai, imagine desert lands with a pop-up city that has amazing high-rise buildings, lots of traffic in and out of the city, and is only a few miles away from the sea.

My aunt and I had gone out one day to do some food shopping, visited an art gallery, and came back to the flat as it started to rain. It was a monsoon. We got a knock on the door from the neighbor from downstairs. Her apartment was flooding, and she asked if we had space for her guest to come stay with us until they could figure out what to do next. She said that she had brought a woman from India who was here to teach a seminar on meditation and stress management, that she was a healer and felt horrible about the weather ruining her stay. Could we help?

We welcomed them in, had a meal together, and all started to share more about who we were. The downstairs apartment was completely flooded at this point, and a reservoir a few miles away had busted, so the streets around us were now flooded. We were not able to leave the apartment; there was no way out. So, we used the confined time in the apartment to learn Villy-Ma's meditation practice. It was what she had flown in for from India, but there was no way she could get to the center to teach the group of women she came in to see. So, we had a private session with her, and it was amazing.

Up until this point, I could not even consider meditation. It was so stressful. Asking me to concentrate on things that don't exist for me and dream about oceans and the waves, blah, blah, blah... it was not for me. I was a total Type-A control freak, so concentration meditation felt like a nemesis to me. I was so wound up. I am so grateful for the practice Villy-Ma taught us because it showed me I was not alone in my distaste for concentration meditation.

"Meditation is to open, release, and fill up the body with light; connect to the divine energy above, which is called 'Mother,' and reach self-actualization/self-realization," she explained.

Villy-Ma shared that we have three energy channels that run through our seven Chakra points in our body. The left is our past, the center is our present, and the right is our future channel. The first six months to a year is focused on the Past Channel. The method allows you to clear blockages from the past in order to step into the present with ease. What I did not realize was how much energy I was still storing in my body from the past that created light blockages from passing through.

I immediately embraced this practice and felt an energy shift after my first session. Villy-Ma told me to practice it when I first wake up and before I go to bed for at least the next six months. I was diligent and did what I was told. In the practice, I would move up the chakra points on the left side of my body with my right hand adding a little pressure and recited a mantra she gave us to repeat for the number of nerve endings on that point. My left hand would be facing the ceiling to receive energy and light through the practice. On the third eye chakra point, which is the center of the forehead, I would cup my right hand and put the weight of my head in my hand and repeat, "I forgive everybody, I forgive everyone," as she instructed me to do. She said to continue repeating this phrase until I felt it in my heart. To just let go and forgive. I was overwhelmed.

I had not learned the depth of forgiveness until this point. I did not realize that when I accepted apologies in the past, I still held onto the story and I did not forgive. I did not let go. I took it all with me. I learned forgiveness is required to be present and live in the now. This meditation practice is a daily habit in my life and one I have been given permission to teach others. It's called Satya Meditation. If you marry daily forgiveness with a daily gratitude practice it will help you stay present and help you break through resistance.

This lesson is about finding alignment between your actions and what you truly believe. Sometimes your actions are based on a place of pain that you are carrying, that will only get you so far if it stems from destruction vs. how to up level your life. I define alignment as the moments we flow through each day feeling connected to everything we do, who we spend time with, and the joy it gives us to live.

Tool #4: Letting Go with Grace

Continue to go through the list of items you identified in the last chapter and give yourself grace as you determine what you must let go of in order to allow new activities that are aligned with your Vision Life goals.

1. *Gratitude:* When you are ready to let something go, I would like you to thank that activity/responsibility for serving you this far. Let it know you are making room for what lifts you up and fills your fulfillment cup. Bless it and release.

2. *Forgiveness:* If some reactions of fear or overwhelm are coming up around not knowing how to let go and align yourself with what you desire, I would like you to forgive the behavior that has held you back.

For example: *Fear, I forgive you for trying to hold me back from my greatness. You protected me for this long from living my large life, and I thank you for that. But it no longer serves me. I appreciate you showing up to make me aware of how bad I want this. You will not lead my decisions. Thank you for fueling them. You can let go of my actions, I've got this!*

Remember, when you have gratitude, fear disappears. If you are finding yourself in overwhelm, find gratitude in your growth spurt. You will soon be aligned and the new habits will start forming.

● ● ● ● ● ●

Another way to achieve this in a daily practice is to create a gratitude journal where you write three to ten things you are grateful for daily. It is a good reminder when you are in moments of doubt, defeat, or struggle, that you always have something to be grateful for. One of my consistent items I am grateful for is water; running water in my house. I had a period of time where we didn't have it for a whole month, and ever since then, I am grateful for every flush. Having gratitude is the easiest gift to give yourself on a daily basis.

CHAPTER 5

I AM SELF-CONFIDENT.

Sometimes when we start to dream big, we lose confidence in what we are capable of because the end goal seems so overwhelming. At this stage of the book, you have now learned the skills on how to break down your goals into smaller activities. With every step you take on that list, you will build even more confidence to go for what you want and let go of what no longer serves you. When you hit resistance you have learned to have gratitude and forgive. See how amazing you are? Do you see how all of these tools build up your self-confidence to go after the life you want? Of course, doubt will creep in; that is a sign you have something to breakthrough! Repeat **I am Self-Confident** when thoughts of self-doubt creep in.

How You Spend Your Time Reflects How BADASS You Really Are!

You are now ready to get into action! By now, you have seen a common theme in my story: if I am not aligning my actions with my calling, an area of my life implodes, and everything I am trying to accomplish suffers. Confidence is key when it comes to focusing on the activities that fill you up, and being clear on what you must say no or not right now to, so you can achieve your Vision Life.

What does an action plan look like? How do you get started and not fall into overwhelm or deception that hinders your momentum? I want to help you be intentional about your steps so the best version of you will shine day in and day out. When I became intentional about how I spent my time and focused on the activities that filled me up, doing the hard work to succeed in the area I was focused on became easier and easier.

A dear colleague of mine once asked how I got so confident and courageous in how I run my life. I define confidence as "Faith in Action." My courage to act comes from faith in my skills, qualifications, what I can offer, and the higher power that guides me. Yes, this can be interpreted into a résumé of experience, but I also am including soft skills like caring for others, being of service, intellect, willingness to learn, willingness to let go, and desire to grow.

At a young age, I realized that it was scarier to not try something new and stay the same than it was to try something new and learn from it. That is all a failure is, a lesson learned to help you try a different way next time or let it go. And when there is success on the other side of trying something new, that is when your confidence is boosted the most. When you can say, "I DID IT!"

In the last few years, I have been doing my best to feel empowered and live in what some refer to as the Stretch Zone. It is the zone right outside of the comfort zone where you inch your way into an area of learning more about yourself, and what you are capable of. I have learned a lot from my work with Tony Robbins training and realized that my limited beliefs around what I am capable of have stopped me from really pushing myself to see what I am made of. Yes, I am an accomplished woman. But as I have shared with you, finding fulfillment in our actions and the ability to pivot when it is not headed in the right direction, is the way I ensure I am living in the Stretch Zone to make sure I am flexing all my muscles.

Every time I came away from a Tony Robbins event, the same story ran through my mind: *Kareen, are you living big enough? Is there a fear that needs to be torn down to break through and be open to more in your life? Are you dreaming big enough? Are you aligned with your Vision Life?*

• • • • • •

In order to stay in the zone, I make sure to surround myself with people who have similar beliefs, teachings, and desire to live their best life. I invest in putting myself in high achiever events and through each move I have made across the country, I try to surround myself with like-minded people. It fills me up!

Sometimes it's hard to navigate what type of person you need to help you sustain the growth you are looking for. The coolest part about the digital age we live in today is that you can find so much content, meet up groups, influencers, and sometimes even family members, that have the energy or skill set you are looking for to up-level your life. I am currently at a point in my life where I can invest a certain amount of my budget to make sure I am in the room with certain people for additional training, however the value I get out of every event I go to is a new connection that inspires me. I also find it in free spaces like a local meet up that is aligned with a part of my life I am passionate about and am able to meet others who have the same drive and passion in that space. All I suggest is to step a little into the Stretch Zone and try to put yourself into new areas to get inspired and motivated to get into action in building a community around you that can fuel how you get to your next destination and not distract you. It is key to staying focused on your goals and achieving them.

• • • • • •

The clearest example of how to participate in the Stretch Zone is through my income goals. As you have read, money has been the backdrop to a lot of lessons learned over the years. My independence and freedom lifestyle depend on my earning potential, so I had to find ways to marry my desired life with different methods of earning. *I learned that without money, you can't do what you want. Plain and simple. Getting your money to earn for you is the best lesson to learn.*

I focused on becoming a six-figure income earner early in my career. Each job search, promotion, and contract I said yes to over the last fifteen years has been with six figures in mind. I visualized it and made it happen. I have certainty in my skillset and the ability to earn, but what has more value to me is the ability to drive impact and contribute to the lives of others. Whether it is through my consulting or coaching practice, I focus on transformation and change to reap the best results. I want to thrive. I want my clients to thrive.

So, I never really focused on setting income or revenue goals past six figures before now. I had a selfish limited belief that resisted leading others or helping others earn income because past stresses of being an executive in the wrong corporate environments resulted in sacrificing myself to earn that income. Being self-employed and moving from contract to contract seemed to fit my desire to be emotionally detached from the outcome and focus on the work. When I lead others, I am fully invested. Their performance represents me as a leader. I would over-extend myself to make sure my direct reports were taken care of, but when it came to managing upwards, I had burned out on working for some leaders who only thought about their personal gains, and could care less about the team helping them make it happen. I avoided building my own company and expanding my offering by expanding my team. It 100% was limiting my revenue and helping others get paid. I didn't want the responsibility or the administrative headaches. I could not believe my fear was leading my income potential. I decided to let it go!

I kicked off 2017 with a seven-figure revenue goal that not only could be lucrative for me but also help build income for others. Challenge accepted! Envision what a seven-figure revenue focus would be so I could prove to myself I am capable, but also stretch myself to figure out how. I would like to know what that feels like. I know I can do so much more and impact more lives if I focus on this goal. I also realized that it is time to stop thinking about the earning model for myself and start considering the other 75% of my skill set, which is helping others earn the income they desire.

And that lit me up! It gave the goal a bigger purpose than me. It was my Why. I followed the steps of this playbook and outlined my Goal, broke down the actions I would need to initiate in Q1 of this year, and got into action.

Here are the goals I had written at the beginning of the year:

Goal: Earn $1M Revenue by 12/31/2017
Action Items:
#1: Lay out all methods of earning and decide which services to maximize to increase income by 01/15/2017.
#2: Connect with members of your network to outline how to leverage your skills/offering and build partnerships to earn income together by 01/30/2017.
#3: Get clear on the services you are offering and start to market them to your network for potential clients by 02/15/2017.

● ● ● ● ● ●

I started with these three goals to get me going. As soon as I completed them, I created a new list of actions to get me closer to the goal. Similar to the steps I gave you earlier in the book, I abide by them myself and put them up on my wall. As I was going through Action Item #1 for this goal, I realized I had several means of income earning I could explore. I decided first to leverage what I had certainty in and what my husband had been telling me for years to do, but was too scared to extend myself this way. I started to source services of other independent contractors through my firm to my clients.

For years, I had worked as a subcontractor for others who made a margin off my time, and I always thought it was a slimy line of business to charge a client twice what you pay the actual contractor for their time. If I was going to extend my services to assist my clients in getting the talent they needed, I wanted to make sure the contractor received the rate they requested (or as close as I could get), and I would increase the rate a little to cover my administrative fees. The contractors were happy, my clients were happy, and I was earning a higher income through my firm.

By June of 2017, I booked over $800,000 in contract revenue using this model. I was at 80% of my revenue goal and it was only halfway through the year! I know you are asking, *How did you do that Kareen? That is insane growth in such a short period of time.* Well, I got focused. I go through the same methods I am sharing with you in this book because it has worked for me year after year; the only difference here is the goal got bigger, but the activities to achieve this goal are the same. Time management is key when you want to achieve your goals, so let me share my favorite method with you. When it comes to exciting new goals, you have to be careful not to abandon what you currently do.

Tool #5: How to make your goals happen: Time Blocking

You can't achieve your goals without knowing where you spend your time. Consistency in the making sure the activities against the goals you have broken down, is required to achieve them as well. Time Blocking is an amazing skill that allows you to ensure you are spending time on the activities that fill you up.

We all have the same 24 hours in the day; let's see how you plan to leverage it to achieve your goals.

A. List the number of hours you are obligated to others right now. Work, Kids Pick Up and Drop Off, Family Care Taking, all the areas where you show up for others. List it out with how many hours a week you spend in those activities.

ACTIVITY	HOURS PER WEEK

B. List the number of hours you spend on self-care, working out, cooking healthy meals, personal appointments, etc.

ACTIVITY	HOURS PER WEEK

C. What is the average number of hours you need to sleep to feel rested each night? Multiply it by 7 = _____.

There are 168 hours available to you every week. Subtract the number of hours you sleep per week = _____. This is the total number of hours you have per week to manage obligatory time and ensure you have the hours devoted to your self care and your goals.

Sometimes it is easier to map it out on a daily calendar and use different colors. Here is an example of something you can create for yourself and use over and over again as things change:

6:30 AM	**Self-Care:** *Meditate, Stretch, Workout*
7:45 AM	**Self-Care:** *Breakfast Shake*
8:00 AM	**Self-Care:** *Get Ready for Work*
9:00 AM	*Start Work*
5:00 PM	*End Work Day*
7:00 PM	*Dinner with Family*
8:00 PM	*Put List of Activities Together for Working Hours Tomorrow*
8:30 PM	*Watch Ted Talk or Funny Show with Husband*
10:30 PM	*Sleep*

Create a grid for yourself and the hours that you plan to work, play and rest. Time block it and see where you can fit your new activities into areas that are not aligned with your current goals. Try it for the next four weeks and see how it goes.

CHAPTER

6

I AM SUCCESSFUL.

You are officially a Badass in Training! We are always evolving, which is where the "in training" comes in. As you introduce yourself to new adventures and experiences to create the Vision Life you desire, just remind yourself your life is a marathon, not a sprint and the one thing you can always control is your attitude on how you show up. You now have a set of tools to lean on and use when you are feeling moments of dissatisfaction or unfulfilled. These methods have gotten me through the lowest moments.

Where I find I celebrate my triumphs the most is when I make the decision to change something that no longer serves me, and push through the doubt, hesitation, and fear knowing that what is on the other side of this growth spurt, is better than where I am in that downer moment. I have to remind myself that **I AM SUCCESSFUL**.

Embracing Success Like a Badass!

As an overachiever, we like to cross things off our list and feel accomplished. I used to weigh success against the achievements until I realized that lead to a world of comparison and competition that did not serve me. I want everyone to succeed. And as you can see, I want to HELP everyone succeed. As I embrace what I have accomplished to date and how it stacks up against my Vision Life, I am successful. I did not always celebrate or appreciate the life I lead, and that is why I have shared those moments with you, too.

Financial success gives me the freedom to decide how I spend my time. I am grateful for that. But it could go in an instant.

I define Badass Success as sustaining an energy no matter what comes my way, where I am true to myself, am free to speak my mind, and can make a choice on how I want to move forward.

Badass Success is being able to share and celebrate moments of joy and fulfillment with those I love. Badass Success is when someone reaches out to me and says, "Kareen, because of you, I..." knowing that all I did was show up for them in a moment of discontent and show them they have options to choose from on how to move forward.

Badass Success is taking a moment to embrace how far you have come and celebrating what you have let go in order to show up in the life you are meant to have, not the one you think you SHOULD have.

I encourage you to define what Badass Success means to you from the intangible space, the emotions around what success feels like, to the tangible space, what it would look like. Get clear on this and make sure you find ways to celebrate your progress along the way. As you have learned by now, purchasing that fabulous diamond pinky ring on Chestnut Street in San Francisco was not for the ring itself, but what it signified for me as a rite of passage through my personal and professional growth journey. Every time I wear it, it reminds me of how far I have come and what a Badass stance I have had to make the life I envisioned come true.

Break Free of Doubt and Know You Are on the Right Track

You now are a Badass at setting and breaking down your goals, and getting into action. I shared with you my simple steps of writing the goal at the top of the sheet and mapping out the top three things you need to accomplish to inch you towards that goal as a start to achieve it. You have now time-blocked how you will put those activities into your daily life to inch towards that goal. What I also suggest is that you put a marker on the calendar (no more than three months out from the start of your action plan) to conduct a Retrospective. This exercise will help you identify your successes and pivot with ease after learning whether the tasks you outlined are aligned with your end goal.

I learned about facilitating Retrospectives in my professional life when I became a Certified SCRUM Master (CSM). For those of you who are not in the world of technology, being a CSM taught me how to facilitate agile teams to deliver high quality products to their customer base by being cohesive, collaborative, and having the ability to pivot with ease when the direction of their work was not in sync with the demands of the client base. A Retrospective is one of the ceremonial meetings that would be facilitated at the end of a segment of development time to check in as a team and apply any changes that would enhance the delivery of the project and team's ability to work together.

I use this with everyone I coach on individual goals, as an assessment tool when I walk into corporate environments to quickly understand what the leadership team thinks is going well and what to improve upon. I also use it on myself when I am trying to achieve my own goals to make sure I am on track and pivot or let go of what is not working with ease.

It's super easy to implement a Retrospective and check in on how you are doing!

Tool #6: Quick and Easy Retrospective to Measure Success and Stay on Track!

Get out a piece of paper and put a line through the center from top to bottom and left to right to create four quadrants.

- **Top Left –** *What have I been doing well? What do I want to continue Doing? What should I celebrate!*
- **Top Right –** *What do I want to stop doing?* Sometimes our goals are super ambition and maybe we need more time, or

maybe we just realize this goal is not the top priority right now, so maybe we need to stop pushing for it, and place something in that is a top priority. Or maybe there are distractions that stop you from focusing on your priorities that you need to let go, delegate or remove...be real!

- **Bottom Left –** *What do I want to start doing?* Now that three months have passed and you may have accomplished everything you set up to on your goals list – this is a time to pull up another set and go through the steps above again to map out what is next, or maybe it is adding the next three priorities against this goal.
- **Bottom Right –** List out the actions you are going to take based on your retrospective of what you have accomplished so far.

Now you have a full cycle of how to dream, map a plan, get into action, and celebrate!

I AM BADASS
AND SO ARE YOU!

When people ask me what I do, I say, "I am a Badass in Training, and I help others become the same." Feel free to start saying that, too. We are not our titles or roles in life; they are just labels. I always get flustered when people would ask me what I do, because I do so many things, but that's not who I am. Saying, "I am a Badass," is so much easier! Following these methods and leveraging this play-book helps me create a Badass Life.

What I love most is helping others achieve their Badass Life! You now have the foundational steps I use with my clients. Every single person I have coached 1:1 or in one of my groups, has had a breakthrough that made them up-level their life, stop questioning who they really are, and step into a deeper realm of self-awareness that has resulted in a higher level of fulfillment in their area of choice. Because of this work, they have earned anywhere from $10,000-$40,000 more annually, built stronger relationships, focused on a deeper spiritual connection through their self-aware-ness work, moved to the city of their dreams, built and run their own kick-ass companies, and my most favorite side effect of this work, helped others by sharing these tools. Now that is another Badass Moment for me!

● ● ● ● ● ●

A recent exchange with one of my executive coaching clients still makes me laugh and shake my head at how bold the words were coming out of my mouth in order to help him wake up and face how he was showing up and how to step into his greatness. We had been working together only two months and already I had helped him identify the gaps in the skill set of his direct reports, the lack of structure and operations across his team, and his need to break old habits of the chief level staff he reported into in order to have the impact he desired. It was a daunting task that required him to really step up and make some hard decisions and get into action. He was overwhelmed, scared, and excited at the same time.

About eight weeks into working together, we were having our one on one session in his office. It was a typical Manhattan office: grey on grey with a window that looked onto another building right across the street. We had just finished a white boarding session where he drew out the layers of service and team structure he envisioned, and he was so clear in his mind on what needed to happen next, but completely unsure of how to go about it. He kept focusing on a limited belief that he could not rock the boat and risk losing his job by proposing his plan to the executive board. He kept saying, "I have only been here six months."

This was probably the tenth time I had heard this excuse and saw his fear as he looked down at the floor, almost cowering away from the leadership life he stepped into and the potentially amazing impact he could make on the firm if he just went for it! But, most of all, I saw him hiding from the man I knew he was inside and was playing into a toxic leadership environment that had gotten used to the status quo and not optimizing newer techniques or technology to enhance their customer experience. He was holding back and not putting himself out there. He was playing small.

I knew he had a vision of achieving the role he was hired into, but it was a stretch for him now that he got it. Self-doubt crept in once he started to understand the hurdles he would have to overcome internally to have the impact and experience working there that he desired. He was unsure of how he could bring what he knew best, which was innovation. He wanted to create new product channels. Most of all, he wanted to break the mold and leave his mark. Now, that is a Badass vision!

I took a deep breath. I stood up and squared my shoulder to align with his; there were about three feet between us. We were facing each other and I looked him straight in the eyes with a serious face and said, "You have been here six months! Enough already, balls out man!" Gasp, did I just say that out loud? Then I remember my fear saying, *Shit, this dude is going to fire me! What did I just say?*

Putting all negative thoughts aside, I continued in the zone of this-is-not-about-me, and I said: "You have been here six months; you know what you need to do to shake things up! You didn't take this job to conform, you took it to challenge yourself and help grow the company. Why are you hiding behind a length of time you have been here? You are the leader of this team. Yes, it is challenging, but if it wasn't, you wouldn't be growing. You are earning this salary for a reason. You got hired for a reason. Balls out man! You have everything you need to do this. What else do you really need to step into your plan if action? The time is now!"

Silence.

I kept my eyes locked on him with assurance in my energy that he had everything he needed to do this. I wish I could have snapped a picture of the change in his stance. He was a little shocked by my word choice, and so was I, but the point was to shake him out of it and it did! He was standing taller, felt more empowered and said to give him two weeks until our next check-in. He was ready to push forward and wanted to have a progress report in our next 1:1 that he could be proud of. It was awesome!

I remember leaving his office shocked he didn't fire me! Who says that? I never said that to anyone before but trusted it was what was needed at the moment. And thank God it worked. He proceeded to send me to his international and west coast offices to assess his leadership teams and help him execute a staffing plan that has helped him not only drive revenue for the firm but also build his reputation as a Badass in his market. He realized he was the only one stopping himself by his limited beliefs and not taking action, he needed to build a kick-ass team to align with his plans.

When he initially found me, he was looking for an Agilest that could help him bring agile practices to his team because he had seen the success of that at his former company. The former CTO at my last firm connected us through email and told him, "I think you need Kareen." The majority of my strategic consulting practice was built on referrals from clients or colleagues I have worked with in the past. When someone a potential new client trusts and recommends you, it is the best way to gain new clients. In my mind, it is the highest form of flattery.

At the time, I was in between gigs, and as I have now shown you, I put together my vision of the type of clients I wanted to attract, the work I wanted to do, and the income I wanted to earn from it. I had a goal of earning $275/hour for my time. My last contract was at $200/hour. The more I understand how third-party vendors started to charge high-end clients a margin for expertise similar to mine, the more I realized I could just ask for that rate myself since that was what the market was paying. I knew this was a stretch, but I had to put the goal out there to see if I could achieve it. Of course, I would have been satisfied with less, but I wasn't going to sell myself short on the next gig, and you never know unless you ask. I had nothing to lose.

After only two thirty-minute conversations with this executive and then his team, he said, "I need you here; I don't care how or under what construct, but I need you here to help guide me on how to build my team and be the leader I need in order to succeed here. So, I am going to bring you in for this project, and I just want you to know what I hope you can help me with once you begin." Normally, there is a proposal phase where I would put the budget out there and it would have to go through the approval process before contracts were signed. I asked him what his budget was and if he wanted me to put together a proposal to discuss rates, and he said, "I will sign off on whatever you propose; I just want you here."

That was a Badass Moment for me. I earned this moment. I manifested it with the same steps I am giving you in this playbook, I had clarity on what I wanted and focused on it. But the real win was I was going to step into the area I love which is to help others achieve their own Badass Moment. He wanted me to be his coach. I was so honored to get paid to do something I absolutely love.

● ● ● ● ● ●

In my leadership and executive coaching practice today, it's the stealth moments like this where I get to be behind the scenes leveraging my ability to unleash, empower, and help evolve the life you want to manifest. This book gives you the baseline skillset to repeat until it becomes habitual and you start to manifest your Vision Life by getting into action. One day, you will wake up and realize that you are living your Badass Life, and your Vision Life is happening right now.

The only person who makes your vision seem like it is off in the distant future is you. Trust in the process and you will see that you have the tools to build your Vision Life right now. As I always say, it is about the journey. I have learned how to celebrate great accomplishments, but what brings me joy is truly being present in the abundant life I have today, and my ability to share my gratitude for all of you letting me be a part of your journey.

LET'S WORK TOGETHER!

I would love to connect with you!

If you are interested in learning more, joining my community of other BITs, live trainings, hearing from me via my monthly newsletter, or even meeting me in person, I invite you to go to www.kareenwalsh.com, join the tribe, and explore the latest way to connect with me.

If you would like to work with me 1:1, feel free to book a session with me through my website!

If you want my workbook, visit my site and request your free copy of the *Be a Badass: Six Tools to Up-Level Your Life Workbook*.

Follow me on Instagram @kareenzwalsh to get the latest on my daily badass habits, and use the hash tags #kzwlifestyle or #beabadassbook if you want me to see your progress in applying the techniques from this book.

Be on the lookout for the next book to leverage: BE A BADASS LEADER. I will be taking all the lessons learned from my own personal executive roles, and my leadership and executive coaching practice and give you the foundational exercises you can apply to become a BADASS LEADER.

Please don't hesitate to share your stories with me, I love hearing from you!

ACKNOWLEDGEMENTS

I would like to thank my parents for being so courageous to come to America in the 1970's from a war-torn country and provide an amazingly abundant life for me. Without their journey, I would not have in order that I am sharing here. I also would probably not have the ambition and drive I do to help other people through hard times, if I did not struggle myself.

I would like to thank my sisters, who ooze with creativity and support when it comes to my new adventures and help me consider all angles of a situation before diving in.

To my husband, my #1 cheerleader, who always says, "You can totally do that!" when I come up with new ventures. It is not easy being married to me and dealing with my constant search for a better version of myself. It takes a great man to support me, lift me up, and grow with me. I love you.

To my inner child, thank you for letting me share our story so we can help others grow and learn ways to heal and step into the Badass version of themselves with ease.

To my coaches, I would not have been able to push through resistance in writing this book and seeing it to completion. To my influencers, Tony Robbins, Lori Harder, Gabby Bernstein, Marianne Williamson, and Lisa Nichols, I want to thank you for putting your work out there so I can learn, grow, and leverage your teachings to share my wisdom with others. Thank you for reminding me it's not about me, it's about how many people I can impact by sharing lessons learned.

To my clients, thank you for allowing me to show up as who I am, give you the best version of myself in each moment we work together, and allowing me to be a part of your journey.

I am blessed to have of your support and encouragement.

- Kareen

CPSIA information can be obtained
at www.ICGtesting.com
Printed in the USA
FFHW011808080119
50101817-54952FF